The Luminous Mysteries

The Luminous Mysteries
Copyright © 2023
Sara Swann

ISBN: 978-1-957344-93-5

Cover design by Mike Parker
Illustrations copyright © 2023 by Sara Swann. Used by permission, all rights reserved.

Published by WordCrafts Press
Cody, Wyoming 82414
www.wordcrafts.net

The Luminous Mysteries

Mysteries of the Rosary for Children
Volume 4

SARA SWANN

WordCrafts Press

To my fourth and final baby, Bitty.
The way you light up a room could be described as luminous.
It is a beautiful blessing to watch your faith blossom.
You make your mama so proud.
I love you to the moon and back!

GETTING STARTED

The first step in praying your Rosary is to get ready. For each mystery below, the prayers you pray will be written in **bold**, so you know what to say, just like the responses you say in Mass, and their Latin translations are there in ***bold italics***, too.

Now, look at your Rosary. Every Rosary has a crucifix, a medallion, six big beads, and 53 smaller beads. All these beads help us pray lots of prayers, and that is just one of the many reasons that make the Rosary so special.

You might be asking, what prayers go where? There are only seven prayers you need to know to pray the Rosary.

1. The Sign of the Cross
2. The Apostles' Creed
3. The Hail Mary
4. The Glory Be
5. The Fatima Prayer
6. The Hail Holy Queen
7. The Final Prayer.

The Sign of the Cross always bookends, or begins and ends, the Rosary just as it begins and ends all our prayers.

The Crucifix is for the Apostle's Creed. The big beads are

for the Our Father prayer, and the small beads are for the Hail Mary. The other prayers are sprinkled throughout.

Are you ready to get started?

Let's go!

THURSDAY

The Luminous Mysteries

During these Luminous Mysteries, we see wonderous acts through Jesus's life. As Pope John Paul II said when he instituted these mysteries, these mysteries show the light of God through Jesus.

Did you know . . .
Pope John Paul II, now Saint John Paul II, prayed all of the decades of the Rosary every day.

Begin with your Rosary in your hand.

Do the Sign of the Cross by touching your Rosary to your forehead, then your chest, then left shoulder, then your right shoulder.

You can remember this because God the Father is in Heaven above us (touch your forehead), God the Son lives in your heart (touch your chest), and Jesus carried the Cross on His shoulders (touch your left shoulder then your right shoulder). When you say amen, put your hands together in front of you, like prayer hands.

In the name of the Father,
> *In nomine Patris,*
>> *(Forehead)*

and of the Son,
> *et Filii,*
>> *(Chest or Heart)*

and of the Holy Spirit.
> *Et Spiritus Sancti.*
>> *(Left then Right Shoulder)*

Amen.
> *Amen.*
>> *(End with prayer hands)*

Now you are ready to begin praying your Rosary. First, hold the Crucifix and pray the Apostles' Creed.

I believe in God,
> *Credo in Deum*

the Father almighty,
> *Patrem omnipoténtem,*

Creator of heaven and earth,
> *Creatórem cæli et terræ.*

And in Jesus Christ,
> *Et in Iesum Christum,*

His only Son,
> *Fílium eius únicum,*

Our Lord,
> *Dóminum nostrum,*

Who was conceived by the Holy Spirit,
> *qui concéptus est de Spíritu Sancto,*

Born of the Virgin Mary,
> *natus ex María Vírgine,*

Suffered under Pontius Pilate,

passus sub Póntio Piláto,

Was crucified, died, and was buried;

crucifíxus, mórtuus, et sepúltus,

He descended into hell;

descéndit ad ínfernos,

On the third day;

tértia die;

He rose again from the dead;

resurréxit a mórtuis;

He ascended into Heaven,

ascéndit ad cælos,

And is seated at the right hand of God,

sedet ad déxteram Dei,

The Father Almighty,

Patris omnipoténtis,

And from there He will come

inde ventúrus

to judge the living and the dead.

est iudicáre vivos et mórtuos.

I believe in the Holy Spirit,

Credo in Spíritum Sanctum,

The Holy Catholic Church,

sanctam Ecclésiam cathólicam,

The communion of Saints,

sanctórum communiónem,

The forgiveness of sins,

remissiónem peccatórum,

The resurrection of the body,

carnis resurrectiónem,

And life everlasting.

vitam ætérnam.

Amen.

Amen.

Now, move your fingers up to the next bead. It is bigger than the other beads and may even be a different color, so you know this bead is for the Our Father prayer.

Our Father, who art in heaven,

Pater noster, qui es in cælis,

hallowed be Thy name.

sanctificétur nomen tuum.

Thy kingdom come,

Advéniat regnum tuum.

Thy will be done,

Fiat volúntas tua,

On earth as it is in heaven.

sicut in cælo, et in terra.

And give us this day our daily bread,

Panem nostrum quotidiánum da nobis hódie,

And forgive us our trespasses,

et dimítte nobis débita nostra sicut

As we forgive those who trespass against us,

et nos dimíttimus debitóribus nostris.

And lead us not into temptation,

Et ne nos indúcas in tentatiónem,

But deliver us from evil.

sed líbera nos a malo.

Amen.

Amen.

Next, we have three small beads. You already know these are for the Hail Mary prayers. Each one of these three beads are special for a different reason. These special beads help open our hearts to be more like Mother Mary in our own *Faith*, *Hope*, and *Charity*.

Did you know . . .
Charity is love?

Move your fingers to the first Hail Mary bead. This Hail Mary bead is the *Faith* bead. We ask for an increase in our Faith as we pray the Hail Mary prayer.

Hail Mary, full of grace,

Ave María, grátia plena,

the Lord is with thee.

Dóminus tecum.

Blessed art thou amongst women,

Benedícta tu in muliéribus,

and blessed is the fruit of thy womb, Jesus.

et benedíctus fructus ventris tui, Iesus.

Holy Mary, Mother of God,

Sancta María, Mater Dei,

Pray for us sinners,

ora pro nobis peccatóribus,

Now and at the hour of our death.

nunc, et in hora mortis nostræ.

Amen.

Amen.

Now, move your fingers to the second small bead. On this bead, we pray the Hail Mary prayer and ask for an increase in our *Hope*.

Hail Mary, full of grace,

Ave María, grátia plena,

the Lord is with thee.

Dóminus tecum.

Blessed art thou amongst women,

Benedícta tu in muliéribus,

and blessed is the fruit of thy womb, Jesus.

et benedíctus fructus ventris tui,Iesus.

Holy Mary, Mother of God,

Sancta María, Mater Dei,

Pray for us sinners,

ora pro nobis peccatóribus,

Now and at the hour of our death.

nunc, et in hora mortis nostræ.

Amen.

Amen.

Finally, move your fingers to the third small bead. On this bead, we pray the Hail Mary prayer and ask for an increase in our *Charity*.

Hail Mary, full of grace,

Ave María, grátia plena,

the Lord is with thee.

Dóminus tecum.

Blessed art thou amongst women,

Benedícta tu in muliéribus,

and blessed is the fruit of thy womb, Jesus.

et benedíctus fructus ventris tui, Iesus.

Holy Mary, Mother of God,

Sancta María, Mater Dei,

Pray for us sinners,

ora pro nobis peccatóribus,

Now and at the hour of our death.

nunc, et in hora mortis nostræ.

Amen.

Amen.

Remember those surprise prayers we talked about earlier? Here is the first time you find them in the Rosary!

With your fingers still on the bead, you say two very special prayers. First, is the Glory Be.

When you say the Glory Be prayer, you bow to the Crucifix to show respect and love to Jesus Christ.

Then, you say the Fatima Prayer. Sometimes, the Fatima Prayer is sometimes called the O My Jesus prayer.

Did you remember . . .
to bow to your crucifix whenever
you pray a Glory Be?

Glory Be

Glória

to the Father,

Patri,

and to the Son,

et Fílio,

and to the Holy Spirit.

et Spirítui Sancto.

As it was in the beginning,

Sicut erat in princípio,

Is now,

et nunc,

And ever shall be,

et semper,

World without end.

et in sæcula sæculórum.

Amen.

Amen.

Then, pray your Fatima Prayer.

O My Jesus,

Dómine Jesu,

Forgive us our sins,

dimitte nobis débita nostra,

And save us from the fires of hell.

salva nos ab igne inferni,

Lead all souls to heaven,

perduc in caelum omnes ánimas,

Especially those in most need of thy

praesertim eas, quae misericórdiae tuae

mercy.

máxime indigent.

Now you're ready to begin your first Luminous Mystery!

The First Luminous Mystery

The Baptism of Jesus

The First Luminous Mystery comes from the Gospel of St. Matthew and tells us why this mystery is important.

And when Jesus was baptized, he went up immediately from the water, and behold, the heavens were opened and he saw the Spirit of God descending like a dove, and alighting on him; and lo, a voice from heaven, saying, 'This is my beloved Son, with whom I am well-pleased.'
St. Matthew 3:16–17

Thoughts to Consider . . .
The fruit of this mystery openness to the Holy Spirit.

Move up to the next big bead. Remember, this is an Our Father bead.

Our Father, who art in heaven,
Pater noster, qui es in cælis,
hallowed be Thy name.
sanctificétur nomen tuum.
Thy kingdom come,
Advéniat regnum tuum.
Thy will be done,
Fiat volúntas tua,
On earth as it is in heaven.
sicut in cælo, et in terra.
And give us this day our daily bread,
Panem nostrum quotidiánum da nobis hódie,
And forgive us our trespasses,
et dimítte nobis débita nostra sicut
As we forgive those who trespass against us,
et nos dimíttimus debitóribus nostris.
And lead us not into temptation,
Et ne nos indúcas in tentatiónem,

But deliver us from evil.

sed líbera nos a malo.

Amen.

Amen.

> **Did you know . . .**
> Jesus was baptized by his cousin, John the Baptist?

Next, pray ten Hail Mary prayers. While you pray think about the Scripture, and also think about the gifts of the Holy Spirit.

Hail Mary, full of grace,

Ave María, grátia plena,

the Lord is with thee.

Dóminus tecum.

Blessed art thou amongst women,

Benedícta tu in muliéribus,

and blessed is the fruit of thy womb, Jesus.

et benedíctus fructus ventris tui, Iesus.

Holy Mary, Mother of God,

Sancta María, Mater Dei,

Pray for us sinners,

ora pro nobis peccatóribus,

Now and at the hour of our death.

nunc, et in hora mortis nostræ.

Amen.

Amen.

> **Pro Tip . . .**
> Move to the next bead each time you say *amen.*

Remember the two special prayers, The Glory Be and The Fatima Prayer, that are hidden throughout our Rosary? You just found them again! Keep holding the tenth bead and pray a Glory Be and a Fatima Prayer. Remember to bow to your Crucifix when you pray your Glory Be.

Glory Be

Glória

to the Father,

Patri,

and to the Son,

et Fílio,

and to the Holy Spirit.

et Spirítui Sancto.

As it was in the beginning,

Sicut erat in princípio,

Is now,

et nunc,

And ever shall be,

et semper,

World without end.

et in sæcula sæculórum.

Amen.

Amen.

Then, pray your Fatima Prayer.

O My Jesus,

Dómine Jesu,

Forgive us our sins,

dimitte nobis débita nostra,

And save us from the fires of hell.

salva nos ab igne inferni,

Lead all souls to heaven,

perduc in caelum omnes ánimas,

Especially those in most need of thy

praesertim eas, quae misericórdiae tuae

mercy.

máxime indigent.

Congratulations! You have just finished praying your first decade of the Rosary! As you prayed, you thought about the gifts of the Holy Spirit, which are wisdom, counsel, understanding, fortitude, knowledge, piety, and fear of the Lord. We receive these gifts at Baptism, at Confirmation, and whenever we ask for them! On the next page, write down some of your thoughts about how the gifts of the Holy Spirit are at work in your life.

> **Can you . . .**
> remember all of the gifts of the
> Holy Spirit?

The Second Luminous Mystery

The Wedding Feast at Cana

The Second Luminous Mystery comes from the Gospel of St. John and tells us why this mystery is important.

On the third day there was a marriage at Cana in Galilee, and the mother of Jesus was there; Jesus also was invited to the marriage, with his disciples.

When the wine failed, the mother of Jesus said to him, 'They have no wine.'

And Jesus said to her, 'O woman, what have you to do with me? My hour has not yet come.'

His mother said to the servants, 'Do whatever he tells you.'

St. John 2:1–5

> **Did you know . . .**
> This is the miracle where Jesus turned the water into wine?

Move your fingers to the next big, Our Father bead.

Our Father, who art in heaven,

Pater noster, qui es in cælis,

hallowed be Thy name.

sanctificétur nomen tuum.

Thy kingdom come,

Advéniat regnum tuum.

Thy will be done,

Fiat volúntas tua,

On earth as it is in heaven.

sicut in cælo, et in terra.

And give us this day our daily bread,

Panem nostrum quotidiánum da nobis hódie,

And forgive us our trespasses,

et dimítte nobis débita nostra sicut

As we forgive those who trespass against us,

et nos dimíttimus debitóribus nostris.

And lead us not into temptation,

Et ne nos indúcas in tentatiónem,

But deliver us from evil.

sed líbera nos a malo.

Amen.

Amen.

Thoughts to Consider . . .

The fruit of this mystery is: "to Jesus through Mary."

Move your fingers along the beads as you pray ten Hail Mary prayers and think about the Scripture.

Hail Mary, full of grace,

Ave María, grátia plena,

the Lord is with thee.

Dóminus tecum.

Blessed art thou amongst women,

Benedícta tu in muliéribus,

and blessed is the fruit of thy womb, Jesus.

et benedíctus fructus ventris tui, Iesus.

Holy Mary, Mother of God,

Sancta María, Mater Dei,

Pray for us sinners,

ora pro nobis peccatóribus,

Now and at the hour of our death.

nunc, et in hora mortis nostræ.

Amen.

Amen.

Keep holding the tenth bead and pray a Glory Be and a Fatima Prayer. Remember to bow to your crucifix when you pray your Glory Be.

Glory Be

Glória

to the Father,

Patri,

and to the Son,

et Fílio,

and to the Holy Spirit.

et Spirítui Sancto.

As it was in the beginning,

Sicut erat in princípio,

Is now,

et nunc,

And ever shall be,

et semper,

World without end.

et in sæcula sæculórum.

Amen.

Amen.

Then, pray your Fatima Prayer.

O My Jesus,

Dómine Jesu,

Forgive us our sins,

dimitte nobis débita nostra,

And save us from the fires of hell.

salva nos ab igne inferni,

Lead all souls to heaven,

perduc in caelum omnes ánimas,

Especially those in most need of thy
praesertim eas, quae misericórdiae tuae
mercy.
máxime indigent.

Did you know . . .
When we ask Mother Mary to pray to Jesus
for us, she does so.

How about that! You have just finished praying your second decade of the Luminous Mysteries of the Rosary!

As you prayed, you thought about how Jesus obeyed Mother Mary when the wedding guests ran out of wine. What do you think of Jesus obeying Mother Mary, and Mother Mary serving as our lifeline to Jesus. Write down some of your thoughts about this mystery on the next page.

The Third Luminous Mystery

The Proclamation of the Kingdom of God

𝒯he Third Luminous Mystery comes from the Gospel of St. Mark.

> **Did you know . . .**
> To proclaim means to tell.

The time is fulfilled, and the kingdom of God is at hand; repent, and believe in the gospel.

St. Mark 1:15

> **Thoughts to Consider . . .**
> The fruit of this mystery is repentance and trust in God. How can you show God that you trust Him?

Move your fingers to the next big, Our Father bead.

Our Father, who art in heaven,

Pater noster, qui es in cælis,

hallowed be Thy name.

sanctificétur nomen tuum.

Thy kingdom come,

Advéniat regnum tuum.

Thy will be done,

Fiat volúntas tua,

On earth as it is in heaven.

sicut in cælo, et in terra.

And give us this day our daily bread,

Panem nostrum quotidiánum da nobis hódie,

And forgive us our trespasses,

dimítte nobis débita nostra sicut

As we forgive those who trespass against us,
> *et nos dimíttimus debitóribus nostris.*

And lead us not into temptation,
> *Et ne nos indúcas in tentatiónem,*

But deliver us from evil.
> *sed líbera nos a malo.*

Amen.
> *Amen.*

Move your fingers along the beads as you pray ten Hail Mary prayers and think about the Scripture. Also think about ways you can show Jesus's love to others.

Hail Mary, full of grace,
> *Ave María, grátia plena,*

the Lord is with thee.
> *Dóminus tecum.*

Blessed art thou amongst women,
> *Benedícta tu in muliéribus,*

and blessed is the fruit of thy womb, Jesus.
> *et benedíctus fructus ventris tui, Iesus.*

Holy Mary, Mother of God,
> *Sancta María, Mater Dei,*

Pray for us sinners,
> *ora pro nobis peccatóribus,*

Now and at the hour of our death.
> *nunc, et in hora mortis nostræ.*

Amen.
> *Amen.*

Keep holding the tenth bead and pray a Glory Be and a Fatima Prayer. Remember to bow to your crucifix when you pray your Glory Be.

Glory Be

Glória

to the Father,

Patri,

and to the Son,

et Fílio,

and to the Holy Spirit.

et Spirítui Sancto.

As it was in the beginning,

Sicut erat in princípio,

Is now,

et nunc,

And ever shall be,

et semper,

World without end.

et in sæcula sæculórum.

Amen.

Amen.

Did you know . . .
Repentance means to be sorry and not do it again.

Now, it's time for the Fatima Prayer.

O My Jesus,

Dómine Jesu,

Forgive us our sins,

dimitte nobis débita nostra,

And save us from the fires of hell.

salva nos ab igne inferni.

Lead all souls to heaven,

perduc in caelum omnes ánimas,

Especially those in most need of thy

praesertim eas, quae misericórdiae tuae

mercy.

máxime indigent.

Great job! You have just finished praying your third decade of the Luminous Mysteries of the Rosary!

As you prayed, you thought about how important it is to turn away from sin and do the will of God. What are some of your thoughts about this mystery? Write down some of your thoughts on the next page.

The Fourth Luminous Mystery

The Transfiguration

The Fourth Luminous Mystery comes from the Gospel of St. Matthew.

And after six days Jesus took with him Peter and James and John his brother, and led them up a high mountain apart. And he was transfigured before them, and his face shone like the sun, and his garments became white as light.
St. Matthew 17:1–2

Thoughts to Consider . . .
The fruit of this mystery is desire for holiness.

Move your fingers to the next big, Our Father bead.

Our Father, who art in heaven,
> *Pater noster, qui es in cælis,*

hallowed be Thy name.
> *sanctificétur nomen tuum.*

Thy kingdom come,
> *Advéniat regnum tuum.*

Thy will be done,
> *Fiat volúntas tua,*

On earth as it is in heaven.
> *sicut in cælo, et in terra.*

And give us this day our daily bread,
> *Panem nostrum quotidiánum da nobis hódie,*

And forgive us our trespasses,
> *et dimítte nobis débita nostra sicut*

As we forgive those who trespass against us,
> *et nos dimíttimus debitóribus nostris.*

And lead us not into temptation,
> *Et ne nos indúcas in tentatiónem,*

But deliver us from evil.
> *sed líbera nos a malo.*

Amen.

>*Amen.*

Move your fingers along the beads as you pray ten Hail Mary prayers and think about the Scripture.

Hail Mary, full of grace,

>*Ave María, grátia plena,*

the Lord is with thee.

>*Dóminus tecum.*

Blessed art thou amongst women,

>*Benedícta tu in muliéribus,*

and blessed is the fruit of thy womb, Jesus.

>*et benedíctus fructus ventris tui, Iesus.*

Holy Mary, Mother of God,

>*Sancta María, Mater Dei,*

Pray for us sinners,

>*ora pro nobis peccatóribus,*

Now and at the hour of our death.

>*nunc, et in hora mortis nostræ.*

Amen.

>*Amen.*

Keep holding the tenth bead and pray a Glory Be and a Fatima Prayer. Remember to bow to your crucifix when you pray your Glory Be.

Did you know . . .
As Christians, we are called to holiness?

Glory Be

Glória

to the Father,

Patri,

and to the Son,

et Fílio,

and to the Holy Spirit.

et Spirítui Sancto.

As it was in the beginning,

Sicut erat in princípio,

Is now,

et nunc,

And ever shall be,

et semper,

World without end.

et in sæcula sæculórum.

Amen.

Amen.

Now, it's time for the Fatima Prayer.

O My Jesus,

Dómine Jesu,

Forgive us our sins,

dimitte nobis débita nostra,

And save us from the fires of hell.

salva nos ab igne inferni,

Lead all souls to heaven,

perduc in caelum omnes ánimas,

Especially those in most need of thy

praesertim eas, quae misericórdiae tuae

mercy.

máxime indigent.

Look how far you've come! You have just finished praying your fourth decade of the Luminous Mysteries of the Rosary!

As you prayed, you thought about how Jesus showed His Glory to three of his Apostles, and about how we should desire the holiness above all else. How do you think Jesus's transfiguration affected the Disciples? How do you think it should affect you? Write down some of your ideas thoughts about holiness on the next page.

The Fifth Joyful Mystery

The Institution of the Eucharist

he Fifth Luminous Mystery comes from the Gospel of St. Matthew.

Now as they were eating, Jesus took bread, and blessed, and broke it, and gave it to the disciples and said, 'Take, eat; this is my body.'

St. Matthew 26:26

Thoughts to Consider . . .
The fruits of this mystery are Eucharistic Adoration and Active Participation in Mass.

Move your fingers to the next big, Our Father bead.

Our Father, who art in heaven,

        Pater noster, qui es in cælis,

hallowed be Thy name.

        sanctificétur nomen tuum.

Thy kingdom come,

        Advéniat regnum tuum.

Thy will be done,

        Fiat volúntas tua,

On earth as it is in heaven.

        sicut in cælo, et in terra.

And give us this day our daily bread,

        Panem nostrum quotidiánum da nobis hódie,

And forgive us our trespasses,

        et dimítte nobis débita nostra sicut

As we forgive those who trespass against us,

        et nos dimíttimus debitóribus nostris.

And lead us not into temptation,

        Et ne nos indúcas in tentatiónem,

But deliver us from evil.

        sed líbera nos a malo.

Amen.

        Amen.

Move your fingers along the beads as you pray ten Hail Mary prayers and think about the Scripture. Think about Jesus and the Apostles at The Last Supper.

Hail Mary, full of grace,

Ave María, grátia plena,

the Lord is with thee.

Dóminus tecum.

Blessed art thou amongst women,

Benedícta tu in muliéribus,

and blessed is the fruit of thy womb, Jesus.

et benedíctus fructus ventris tui, Iesus.

Holy Mary, Mother of God,

Sancta María, Mater Dei,

Pray for us sinners,

ora pro nobis peccatóribus,

Now and at the hour of our death.

nunc, et in hora mortis nostræ.

Amen.

Amen.

Keep holding the tenth bead and pray a Glory Be and a Fatima Prayer. Remember to bow to your crucifix when you pray your Glory Be.

Glory Be

Glória

to the Father,

Patri,

and to the Son,

et Fílio,

and to the Holy Spirit.

et Spirítui Sancto.

As it was in the beginning,

                    Sicut erat in princípio,

Is now,

                           et nunc,

And ever shall be,

                        et semper,

World without end.

            et in sæcula sæculórum.

Amen.

                        Amen.

Now, it's time for the Fatima Prayer.

O My Jesus,

                    Dómine Jesu,

Forgive us our sins,

            dimitte nobis débita nostra,

And save us from the fires of hell.

              salva nos ab igne inferni,

Lead all souls to heaven,

            perduc in caelum omnes ánimas,

Especially those in most need of thy

        praesertim eas, quae misericórdiae tuae

mercy.

                máxime indigent.

You are almost finished praying your first entire Luminous Mysteries of the Rosary!

Pro Tip . . .
We celebrate this at every Mass!

As you prayed, you thought about The Last Supper with Jesus. How must it have felt being the first Christians to adore Jesus and partake of the Eucharist? Write down some of your ideas about how the Apostles felt on the next page.

The Mystery of the Rosary

The Ending of Each Mystery

The ending of each Mystery of the Rosary consists of two very special prayers: The Hail Holy Queen and The Final Prayer.

Hail Holy Queen

Hail Holy Queen,

Salve Regína,

Mother of Mercy,

mater misericórdiæ;

our Life, our Sweetness, and our hope.

vita, dulcédo, et spes nostra, salve.

To thee we cry,

Ad te Clamámus

poor banished children of Eve.

éxsules fílii Evæ;

To thee we send up our sighs,

Ad te Suspirámus,

mourning and weeping in this valley of tears.

geméntes et flentes in hac lacrimárum valle.

Turn then most gracious advocate,

> *Eia ergo, Advocáta nostra,*

Thine eyes of mercy toward us,

> *Illos tuos misericórdes óculos ad nos convérte:*

and after this, our exile,

> *Et Iesum, benedíctum fructum*

show unto us,

> *ventris tui, Nobis post hoc exsílium*

the blessed fruit of thy womb, Jesus.

> *osténde.*

O clement, O loving, O sweet Virgin Mary.

> *O clemens, o pia, o dulcis Virgo María.*

Pray for us O Holy Mother of God,

> *Ora pro nobis, Sancta Dei Genetrix.*

that we may be made worthy

> *Ut digni efficiamur*

of the promises of Christ.

> *promissiónibus Christi.*

Amen.

> *Amen.*

The Final Prayer ends each Mystery of the Rosary.

Let us pray.

> *Oremus.*

O God, whose only begotten Son,

> *Déus, cújus Unigénitus*

by His life, death, and resurrection,

> *per vítam, mortem, et resurrectiónem*

has purchased for us the

> *Súam nóbis salútis*

rewards of eternal life,

> *ætérnæ præmia comparávit:*

grant, we beseech Thee,

concéde, quæsumus:

that meditating upon these mysteries

ut hæc mystéria

of the Most Holy Rosary of

sacratíssimo beátæ

the Blessed Virgin Mary,

Maríæ Vírginis Rosário recoléntes,

we may imitate what they contain

et imitémur quod cóntinent,

and obtain what they promise,

et quod promíttunt, assequámur.

through the same Christ Our Lord.

Per eúndem Chrístum Dóminum nóstrum.

Amen.

Amen.

Remember what bookends all your prayers—including your Rosary prayers—The Sign of the Cross.

In the name of the Father,

In nomine Patris,

(Forehead)

and of the Son,

et Filii,

(Chest or Heart)

and of the Holy Spirit.

Et Spiritus Sancti.

(Left then Right Shoulder)

Amen.

Amen.

(End with prayer hands)

Acknowledgements

There are so many I would like to thank for helping the Mysteries of the Rosary for Children series come to fruition. My children, who not only stood by me as I taught myself to draw and then to paint in order to create the illustrations for this series, but drew and painted right along with me. My parents, who not only encouraged this project from the beginning, but were just as excited as me as each painting progressed and came to *life*. To my publishers, Mike and Paula, as they championed this project from the beginning, deep within the throes of the pandemic.

> *And the angel said to them: Fear not; for, behold, I bring you good tidings of great joy that shall be to all the people. For today, a Savior has been born for you in the city of David: he is Christ the Lord. And this will be a sign for you: you will find the infant wrapped in swaddling clothes and lying in a manger. And suddenly there was with the Angel a multitude of the celestial army, praising God and saying, Glory to God in the highest, and on earth peace to men of good will.*
>
> *St. Luke 2:10-14 NIV*

Sara Swann-Barnard BSN, RN

ABOUT THE AUTHOR

Sara Swann loves to write and has more than thirty credited works available in print.

She holds a Bachelor of Arts degree in History and spent several years as a teacher in West Texas before earning a Bachelor of Science degree in Nursing. She now works as an emergency room nurse in Houston, Texas, where she, her children, and their menagerie of rescue pets—six in all—make their home.

In her spare time, Sara and her family enjoy ice cream and the beach, but she wishes someone who majored in Physics and Engineering would hurry up and invent a time machine so she could meet St. Francis of Assisi, Henry VIII, William Wallace, and Vlad the Impaler.

Connect with Sara online at:

www.NurseSaraBooks.com